Information Is Not Knowledge

7 Key Strategies for Retirement

Bob Drake

Information Is Not Knowledge

Published by:
90-Minute Books
Newinformation Inc
302 Martinique Drive
Winter Haven, FL 33884
www.90minutebooks.com

Published in the United States of America

ISBN-13: 978- 0692476611
ISBN-10: 069247661X

Here's What's Inside...

Birmingham, MI
August, 2015

One of the things people often ask me is where the market is headed. They want the secret to being able to time the market. Over and over I explain to them that <u>no one</u> can predict the market successfully. No one. That doesn't mean you need to leave your retirement to chance however. Far from it.

Effective money management involves two important components: managing your investments and planning for your future. You need both of these for retirement. But the financial world is filled with pundits and experts all claiming the sky is falling at 5 o'clock and then the opposite at 6 o'clock. How does one differentiate the hype when the hype is so prevalent?

That's why I wanted to write this book. What follows is the transcript where I walk you through my seven financial strategies for retirement. I share with you why information is not knowledge, why your retirement is so vastly different than your parents and grandparents' retirement and what to do about it.

Enjoy the Book!

I hope this book educates you about how to approach your retirement and encourages you to put key strategies in place to help avoid the mistakes a lot of people make when it comes to their retirement.

To Your Success!

Bob Drake

Bob Drake offers securities through Sigma Financial Corporation. Member FINRA/SIPC.

295 Elm Street, Suite 2
Birmingham, MI 48009

Information Is Not Knowledge!

Susan: Good afternoon. This is Susan Austin and I'm excited to be here with Bob Drake. Bob is going to be sharing with us his thoughts and ideas on why information is not the same as knowledge and how to prepare for retirement. Welcome, Bob.

Bob: Thank you, Susan, glad to be here.

Susan: Why did you want to write a book on helping people get to retirement successfully?

Bob: There's a lot of misinformation out there on what to do and what not to do when it comes to retiring well, and I felt it was time to try to get the good word out there. I want to help get people on the right track—get them some clarity and some confidence.

You see, there are tons of information on what to do with your money; it can be overwhelming. Everybody has vast resources for getting information on mutual funds and investments. The trick comes in knowing how to implement that information and what information is appropriate for their personal situation.

Having too much information can sometimes be detrimental. It can paralyze somebody and then, out of fear, they don't take any action. They will come into my office and tell me, "I read you should do this," or, "somebody told me this piece of information", and so instead of taking action, it just paralyzes them and nothing happens.

The problem is getting more elevated now due to technology and social media and financial stations that are blaring on the television 24 hours each day, 7 days a week. If you want to hear the markets are going to go down, you can find that information. If you want to hear the markets are going to go up, you'll find that information also. My goal here is to get people to cut through all the clutter that's out there and allow them to take action in a confident manner. So they are sure where they want to go and how to get there.

Why Don't More People Retire Well?

Susan: I can see where this is a problem. Let's talk about why more people don't have the retirement they want. You would think in today's modern world, this wouldn't be an issue.

Bob: That's a good point. There are many great plans or products that are available to help people reach their retirement goals, but the average person on the street doesn't know which path is right for them. Everyone's situation is different, so it's hard to discern which applies to them. People have many things going on—family life, jobs, careers—which take up a lot of their time nowadays. So it becomes an issue of a lack of attention or effort, which causes them to get to retirement without the necessary funds.

People worry that their money will run out. They want their money to last as long as they do. Statistics[1] show that if you have a married couple, both age 65, there's a 50% chance that one of those partners will live to age 92. With people living so much longer today than they did a generation

[1] U.S. Annuity 2000 Mortality Table, Society of Actuaries

ago, having your money last a long, long time is very important.

The old notion of somebody getting to retirement and it's time to be really conservative, may not work as well in today's world, just because of the longer life expectancies. They could be living in retirement 20 to 30 years or longer; that's a long time-horizon.

The old model was: retire at age 65, put all your savings and investments into very conservative products or plans, and that would carry you on long enough to make it through your retirement years. But people weren't living as long back then. Maybe someone would live five or ten years after retirement. Just that difference of having to stretch your money another 10 or 20 years, changes the whole planning process.

We need a new model from which to work. In fact, some people may be living longer in retirement than they are in their working years. Some insurance companies are actually designing their products to last until age 120. If insurance companies are designing products to last that long, this is a very legitimate concern and topic.

Why Time Is More Important than Timing

Susan: When do they need to know to get to plan well for retirement?

Bob: I think at the top of the list would be that they have confidence in their financial situation, meaning they know that they're going to be able to pay their bills month after month. They know that their money is designed to last for a long period of time.

They know that they have some money set aside for unexpected events that creep up on everybody. Confidence leads to clarity. When someone has a plan, they become clear on the direction they're heading.

Susan: With us living so much longer than in the past, do you think that the model of saving 10% of what you earn still applies for the younger generation that is just starting in the workforce now?

Bob: To some extent it is; saving 10% of income is a good rule of thumb to start. They also need to be aware that the old traditional plans like pensions and employers taking care of their employees' retirement needs are not really in existence anymore. All the planning, all the risk is now on the employee, the individual. They've got to set aside the money. They've got to choose how it's invested. The employer, other than providing a plan for the employee to do that, isn't really involved in that much more.

I run across a lot of clients who are in their 50s or 60s, and their kids are just starting out their careers. The parents are constantly nudging the kids, "Hey, start putting money aside in your IRA or your 401(k)." Because they're young and they don't necessarily see how it all works, they keep postponing it. "Oh, I'll get to it. I'll start later. After we do this or that." That can be a mistake. Time is more important than timing.

Susan: What do you mean by that?

Bob: The more time you're able to save money and invest in the markets is more important than waiting for a certain event to happen, or timing the markets:

are they high or are they low, is this a good time to invest? The time in the market is more important than timing the market.

When you're in your early 20s and you've never had any experience with picking stocks and all of a sudden, you have to determine if you are aggressive or conservative, they throw all kinds of investment lingo at you about what different types of funds are available. How is somebody supposed to make a good choice, an educated decision with what little information they have? It's certainly challenging. Very often they often just guess at it.

7 Financial Strategies for Retirement

Susan: Walk us through what the reader needs to know to retire with enough money.

Bob: I've put together the seven strategies that an individual can adopt to plan for a successful retirement. Following these strategies doesn't guarantee anything of course.

Strategy One: Understand The Money Time-Horizon

The first strategy would be, understanding the time-horizon of the money. Saving for retirement to be 20 to 30 years is certainly a normal time-horizon nowadays. When I'm sitting down and planning for a client, that's the viewpoint that I always have. We've got to plan for this money to last 30 years.

When a person is just starting out their career, they certainly have a long time to save, and since they have a long time until they need the money, they might be able to take a more aggressive or growth-oriented position. Somebody who's starting out their retirement still has the long time-horizon, but because they're using this money as an income stream, they have to be more careful about being positioned too aggressively or too conservatively.

Strategy Two: Why It is Important to Understand Your Risk Tolerance

The next strategy is a direct result of our always-rising inflation and cost of living. Some investments are not even keeping up with cost of living adjustments each year. If you don't carefully manage your investments, 1) you may not get any return on your money, 2) you may be taking money out of your account, and 3) you may not even be keeping up with inflation. Next thing you know, you may have a big downward spiral of your money, and that could lead to running out of money a lot sooner than one expects.

Susan: It's a tricky balance that you're encouraging here.

Bob: It is a tricky balance. Getting some professional guidance, from my perspective, is one way to help combat that

Susan: Is there a direct correlation between risk and return?

Bob: It doesn't have to be an extreme correlation on either side; there is a happy medium.

Susan: People have to understand their risk tolerance.

Bob: Right. In the planning process there are some tests you can take—for lack of a better word—to try to help you find out where you fit into this level of risk. Are you an aggressive investor? Are you conservative? Are you somewhere in the middle? There are ways to help you figure out where your comfort level is.

These tests take into account not only a person's age and their time-horizon until they need to use the money, but also some of their personal feelings about how they feel when the market is up. How do you feel when the market is down? Does that concern you over a three-month period? Does that concern you over a five-year period? Based on all those different pieces of the puzzle, that's where you can start designing a plan that's sort of tailor-fit to that individual situation.

Susan: Do you find people's inclinations change overtime?

Bob: They do. No question about it.

Susan: How often should someone revisit this?

Bob: Every few years would be worst-case scenario. With my clients, I like to do it on an annual basis. Situations change—markets change, personal views change, actual situations change. You can't just design a financial plan and put it on the shelf for 30 years.

Strategy Three: Don't Ignore Your Money

This leads us to the next strategy: don't ignore your money. This means don't just put it someplace and totally forget about it and never look at it again, or look at it every couple of years or something. You've got to pay attention to the investment environment that's out there.

Susan: What are people doing with their money when they get to retirement? They're not leaving it in the risky investment, are they?

Bob: Their portfolios might be a little bit riskier than they used to be 15–20 years ago. The plus side of that is that, generally, the riskier investments also give one potential for keeping up with inflation, which is certainly a big factor. It also gives one potential for growth of their money. There are some pluses to that. However, there is also a greater risk of losing your money in a riskier investment.You just have to be conscious of the risk involved.

Susan: Are there new options for them?

Bob: There are some insurance products out there that do provide a guaranteed income stream: no matter whether the markets are up or down, you'll still get your same income stream each month. Those types of programs are warranting a lot of conversation in today's environment. It doesn't mean that they're perfect or right for everybody, but they certainly need to be discussed.

Strategy Four: Know How to Distribute Your Money

Susan: Talk to us about knowing how to distribute your money. Since we are living so long, does that mean we need a new plan to access our money?

Bob: This strategy ties into the last one, and that's finding that suitable mix of investments. And yes, that can change over time, again based on personal situation and changes, it's probably the biggest thing. You might go into retirement and have a very nice long life expectancy, so we have to design a plan to last 30 years. But if, all of a sudden, an illness creeps in, that can certainly change the time-horizon that money's needed, which can change how we try to allocate things.

Susan: Is there a rule of thumb that people can follow?

Bob: I think the websites and the media folks periodically try to put out some rules of thumb. I don't know how realistic they are or if they truly work. I think it's different for every individual. It's not like every person at age 70 should have this type of portfolio because one person's situation is going to be different than his neighbor, who is also age 70.

Susan: But what about withdrawing the money? Is there a rule of thumb on how to best access that?

Bob: Yes, there are some rules of thumb there around what they call "withdrawal rates". What percent of your assets are you withdrawing each year? Some common withdrawal rates could be 4% a year, or maybe 5% a year.

Susan: Do you find that generally to be true with your clients?

Bob: One retirement account option is an IRA account, an individual retirement account. There are many things you can use to fund your IRA—stocks, bonds, mutual funds, an annuity, CD at the bank. With an IRA, you pay income tax on the amount of money that you take out of it each year. So that's a very powerful concept. Of course the downside is if you withdrawal the money early, there can be penalty and fees, so again, speaking with a professional to discuss their situation is advised.

Strategy Five: Ignore the Media

Susan: That's very helpful. Let's talk about your next strategy, which is "Ignore the Media" - what do you mean by that?

Bob: The media is trying to get you to listen to their station, watch their TV program, and buy their magazine. That's their real goal, so they're going to sensationalize every piece of news or data point that's out there, and that goes back to what I said earlier about people ending up paralyzing themselves, "I heard this, I heard that, I don't know what to do, so I'm not going to do anything." And, again, with these news channels broadcasting 24 hours a day, websites, Twitter—all the different types of media—the information is just overwhelming. The phrase I use is noise. Most of it is just a bunch of noise. It's just causing confusion. It's not really getting the true message out there of what's going on.

Susan: How does someone get the true message without getting bogged down with the hyped-up media?

Bob: By tapping into some reliable sources, and that would be one, are the financial advisors of the world. That's our job, to cut through all that noise, keep our clients on track, and keep them from making emotional decisions; to hold their hands along the way and keep them on the path. Other trusted sources could be, for example, information from some of the larger mutual fund families.

Strategy Six: Don't Try To Predict the Direction of the Market

On predicting the market, the question I get all the time is, "When's the market going to go down?" Who knows? Nobody has that answer. NO ONE has been able to predict the market on a consistent basis. The market goes up, just not in a straight line. It never has and never will.

We'll know when the market starts to go down. People will start commenting, "I heard this piece of news on the radio today, and so does that mean the markets are going to go up?" Well, time will tell. You can't really make those predictions from an advisor's standpoint. That being said, we do have some tools and research capabilities that are available to us so we can see some of the trends that are out there, whether they're up or down, and we can follow those trends. But that's different than predicting whether the market's going to go up or down. We're following what the market's telling us, and when the market tells us it's going to go in a different direction, that's when we adjust accordingly.

If you're monitoring the market like we do or have some of these research capabilities, you can start to see some of the trends so that maybe you can avoid. There is no perfect plan. You will never time the market perfectly at the top. You'll never time it perfectly at the bottom. If you can catch the major trends, then you're going to be in good shape and when that one trend ends, there'll be another trend that's out there developing. Follow that trend.

Susan: Reminds me of the real estate industry when people tried to predict where that is heading as well.

Bob: It's the same thing. When it's all hot, everybody thinks that they can do it or flip houses and those types of things. All of a sudden it ends, and everybody quits doing that and moves on to the next thing.

Susan: If the market is trending downward, what do you suggest they do with their money?

Bob: There are many different strategies for managing risk in your portfolio. In my firm, I use five model portfolios, ranging from an aggressive model to a conservative model. I call the aggressive model a model five, and the most conservative model is a model one. Let's say things are going along normally in the markets and you're in a model three, then, all of a sudden, we start getting some indication that the trend is going to change to the downside. Now we can move from a three to a two or down to a one just to help manage market risk. And if the trend starts to go back up, then you can move from the model one or two back up to your normal number three.

These are longer term trends, so they're more gradual. That's the definition of the difference between following the trend and timing the market. Folks who are timing the market, are trying to buy an individual stock based on where it was today versus 2:00 tomorrow afternoon and more short-term type things. That's just crazy stuff.

Strategy Seven: Don't Ignore Your Portfolio

As you can see, a lot of these things kind of tie into each other. But don't just create your plan and put it on the shelf and stick your head in the sand. Eventually, something is going to change, whether it's the markets or your personal situations, and your retirement plan should be able to adjust with you.

Susan: As you mentioned earlier, at least once a year, they should be paying close attention to this.

Bob: Definitely, and that's from a personal standpoint. If you're working with an advisor, I would hope the advisor is watching it on a much more consistent basis. That doesn't mean that everything is going to be timed perfectly, but at least they're paying attention to it on a more regular basis.

Why Information Is Not Knowledge

Susan: Why do you call the book "Information is not knowledge?" Can you elaborate on that?

Bob: The information's all there. Information is a few clicks away on a keyboard or phone. We can all look at the same information on a website about a particular mutual fund and see its rate of return, its holdings, and how long it's been around. But having the knowledge to know what that really means and how to integrate that into your own portfolio or personal situation, that's where the experience of an advisor who's got some training and education in these types of things can help determine if that really is the right fit for you.

An example of this is when someone is bragging about some hot stock tip they have around the water cooler. You'll hear people touting a particular mutual fund and some Biotech stocks that most people have never heard of. If you're in retirement, you might get some big returns, but all of a sudden, if that particular sector goes south, that could really hurt your portfolio in a very short time-horizon. At this stage, is that really an appropriate piece in your investment portfolio?

My compliance department reminds me I need to point out that past performance is no guarantee of future performance or results.

Mistakes to Avoid When Planning For Retirement

Susan: Good point. Are there mistakes that you see people make when they are approaching retirement or get into retirement that you'd like to highlight?

Bob: Probably, one of the biggest mistakes when approaching retirement is addressing it too late. People who call me two months before they get ready to retire and say they want to retire and they want to sit down and do the planning, that scares me. You've got to start early and be on it for a long period of time.

Susan: When should they be making that appointment, Bob?

Bob: Five to ten years before you want to retire is when you have to start putting a little more serious thought into it. "Hey, ten years away. Okay, what's the path I'm on? Have I been saving enough? Have

I earned a certain rate of return on my money? I've got this amount saved up and I put aside this amount each year for the next few years, how much money will that accumulate to?" Well, that's a great place to start. Part two of that should be, "Well, now that I've got this big sum of money, how much income is that going to create for me each year?" Is that enough for you to take care of what you need to take care of?

Common Myths in the Financial Planning Industry

Susan: What are some of the myths in the financial planning industry today that have perpetuated through the years?

Bob: Cheap does not mean better. There's a lot of publicity out there about making sure you've got "super low-cost funds". There's nothing wrong with having low costs, but that's not the point

What I mean by this is, there's a cost to own all mutual funds. And in that context, they're totally correct.

But just because a mutual fund has low cost, doesn't mean it's had better results or a better rate of return, than a fund which might cost a little bit more. The mutual fund's prospectus can provide a summary of the fees and expenses.

How to Prepare for Your Retirement

Susan: If someone has questions about their individual situation, Bob, how can they get in touch with you?

Bob: The first step would be to check out our firm's website, which is http://www.drakefinancialservices.com. There, you'll see some videos of me to get my perspective on a few things and my demeanor. It will also walk someone through our unique process that we've developed, called the Financial Advocate Approach. And then certainly, they can call directly to the office and request to talk with me or even arrange a time to sit down, meet and talk.

Susan: Can you share for the reader what the Financial Advocate Approach is?

Bob: It's a four-step process that I've developed where we continually address a client's needs and situation, so that we're not skipping any steps when we sit down for a review, and we don't forget to ask questions about future planning needs. It's a revolving four-step process that we run through with every client. We think we're pretty good at it and pretty thorough at it to help our clients reach their goals.

Susan: Are you able to meet with them at any stage in the process, meaning when they are first starting out and those who are close to retirement?

Bob: Oh, definitely. We have clients of all ages, from those just starting out to clients well within their retirement years. But the four steps in our process are the same for everybody. Certainly, the answers to the questions might be different and the plans implemented might be different, but the same four steps are followed for everybody.

Susan: I want to thank you, Bob, because I think you're highlighting a huge point here. What I'm taking away from this is that, even if I was someone who was intelligent and wanted to make it a hobby to follow the market and kind of get involved, there are so many layers to this and so much information, as you said, but that doesn't mean that someone's going to compile that into the right portfolio. And I'm assuming, if they sit down with you and go through these four steps, the end result is that they will have the knowledge, not just the information.

Bob: Correct. We have many clients who come in and make comments that they get overwhelmed just looking at quarterly statements for their accounts and what all the numbers and some of the different phrases mean.

There's a lot of jargon, and a lot of folks just flat out say they don't have an interest in this. They don't have the time to deal with it because they're taking care of their families and careers, and that's where they need some help from someone.

Susan: Right, someone like you.

Bob: Someone like me, that's right.

Susan: All right. I want to thank you, Bob. This has been very enlightening.

Bob: The first step of reaching out and getting an outside viewpoint is key. The truth will set you free.

Here's My Retirement Planning Strategy...

People are living longer than ever before. Your money in retirement has to last you 20 or even 30+ years. The confusing part is not knowing the strategies that may be suitable to your short and long term needs.

That's where we come in. We help people just like you plan and invest their money toward their retirement goals.

Step 1: We invest 60 minutes having a conversation about your vision for a financial future, and establish a framework for moving forward together.

Step 2: We transform your vision into a measurable plan. Our Strategic Wealth Plan allows us to outline the exact financial solutions we have tailored to meet your financial objectives.

Step 3: We take it from here and design and implement your Strategic Wealth Plan. We review the results with you on an ongoing basis and establish new goals.

If you'd like us to help, just send an email to: rdrake@sigmarep.com and we will take it from there.